Getting Started in Freelance Writing

By Ginny Simon

Dedication

I dedicate this book to Joan Blumberg, who gave me the opportunity to develop and teach Freelance Writing university-level class with her. The curriculum formed the basis for this book. I would also like to dedicate the book to all the current – and future – freelancers who work to make this lifestyle a fulfilling career.

Acknowledgements
Thanks to my sharp-eyed editors including Linda Barba, Daria Killinger, Danielle Myers, Lila Roomberg, Diane Warchola and Joan Blumberg. And many thanks to Corner Office books for their support and for the opportunity to bring this project to light. It takes a village.

Published 2017 by Corner Office Books
Printed in the United States of America

ISBN: 0-9980899-6-6
EAN-13: 978-0-9980899-6-6

Cover art and design by Dwayne Booth

Table of Contents

Introduction

Do you ever find yourself wanting to scratch a creative itch? To be your own boss, with control of your time? To learn about different businesses, people and the world in general? Freelance writing may be for you.

Freelance writers are individuals who work on different writing assignments for different clients. They are typically self-employed, control their own schedule, and experience the same ups and downs as any business. Sound like fun?

There are lots of pros to freelance writing. Working in your pajamas is a biggie for many people. They envision working at home, putting in a load of laundry when needed and getting dressed only to go to the post office to collect the checks.

That's only part of the story, however, and a small part at that. It doesn't take into account the hard parts of getting assignments, keeping the business, and getting more business. It doesn't consider the inevitable distractions at home – from the dog with a tennis ball to the phone, children, or a friend who wants to take you to lunch. The list goes on—even if you work at a local coffee shop.

Suppose you are a self-motivated individual with great ideas that you know will appeal to many online and offline publications. That's great – and it's necessary. But not yet sufficient.

To be a successful freelance writer – at least without running afoul of the law, you also have to know a bit about business (more about that later in the book). You have to know how to keep records and, if you don't want to have to hire a bookkeeper, you have to know how to categorize and track your income and expenses. You will have to do your own billing and your own collections (yes, some people just don't pay on time), and file tax returns.

Freelance writing can be a great way to live—working on interesting and diverse assignments, managing your own time, being your own boss and, of course, working in your slippers. Be mindful though that these perks only come after you've had some successes. Getting there can be tough. Do you have what it takes?

Ask yourself:

- Are you self-motivating? Working at home can be distracting with life pulling your attention away from the task at hand.

- Can you stick to deadlines? This is critical to developing the quality of relationships you need to get repeat business.
- Do you enjoy research? While some writers can make a good living working in a specific niche, most write on many topics. You need to understand and enjoy the research that will make your articles accurate and credible.
- Do you enjoy working with different people (editors, interviewees, etc.) and can you deal effectively with the occasional difficult personality?
- Are you organized? Simultaneous assignments, while that's often good news, require good time management.
- Are you ready to tackle the business aspect of freelancing? It is a business after all, so you will need to keep accurate records, invoice in a timely manner, and basically, conduct yourself professionally.
- Are you a goal-setter? Meeting simple goals, such as sending five emails a week to prospective clients, adding six ideas to your idea folder every month, drafting four queries a month, can help build your freelance business.
- Can you support yourself as you build your business? This is not unique to freelancers. Anyone starting a business must consider the economics of how to live until the money starts to roll in.

- Can you work on your own? Freelancing can be lonely.

Getting started is challenging. I started part-time, while maintaining my full-time job and gradually moved to full-time freelancing. Your approach will depend on your financial situation and how much time and effort you can devote to building your business (see Chapter 8 on Marketing). Stay serious and stay focused. It can be a good life.

Chapter 1
Freelance Opportunities

Magazines both online and off, newspapers and blogs are obvious possibilities but just the tip of the iceberg. Some of these opportunities can be lucrative, others less so. But they all should be considered because few freelancers make a living from just one market.

Many freelancers write for small, local businesses or publications. It's a start. They don't pay a lot but it does help build your portfolio. Bottom line is that small businesses have small budgets. If you're just getting started, smaller outlets will be easier to break into and may be key to building your portfolio. The truth is, though, that bigger is often better.

So, get your start where you can, but set your sights high.

Publications
Publications, both online and off-line are the obvious go-to marketplace. They range from local publications directed to a geographic market, for instance, seniors or parents to top consumer magazines.

Most still offer a print edition as well as online content. Often online publications will use additional content not available in the print edition, simply because they can. This can mean additional income for you.

Consumer magazines are a major source of income for many writers. These magazines target everything from family and children, hobby-focused publications for every sport, craft, music, health, money, lifestyle and many, many more.

Finding appropriate target publications among the thousands that are out there can sound intimidating but is likely to be easier than you think. *Writer's Market* is one of the best sources, with hundreds of listings for book publishers, magazines, literary agents, and more. Most listings include the publication name and contact information, an editorial contact, circulation, what they do and do not accept, and payment terms. It is, in my opinion, an invaluable source for freelancers.

Other resources include:

- Writersweekly.com
- TheWriteLife.com
- freelancewritinggigs.com
- woodenhorsepub.wordpress.com

This is far from a complete list but it's a start.

If there are specific areas in which you are particularly interested, try Googling them with the word "magazines" or "publications" after it. If you are interested in writing about aviation, for instance, a search of aviation magazines will yield many online and off-line outlets.

Business to business publications are another big outlet. B2B, as marketers call it, is marketing from one business to another, such as legal or accounting services to companies or kitchen equipment manufacturers to restaurants. These publications, typically with a small staff, are often looking for articles with good content. Bad news? They don't pay very much. But if you are working for a corporate client that is marketing to other businesses and might benefit from having their company name appear in one of these publications, this can be a lucrative way to go.

In fact, vertical trade publications are the bread and butter for many freelancers. There are magazines for every industry, usually more than one. Publications for the utility industry, for instance, include *Pipeline & Gas Journal Magazine, Water Technology Magazine, Power Engineering Magazine, and Water Finance & Management* - to name just a few. The list goes on for pages. Every industry has at least one—probably more—publication. If you have a background in a particular industry, it may be a good place to start.

Associations often have their own publications as well so research relevant groups and see if they have a magazine or newsletter and whether or not they accept freelance material. A good relationship with an association can also result in additional business such as press releases, newsletter articles, social media posts and more. If you do a good job, they can also refer you to members who may have a need for an article or press release. Sometimes an association member will want to contribute an article to the association's magazine but doesn't have the staff or time internally to get it done. In my years working with an insurance marketing association, referrals have turned into significant business.

Another thought regarding articles. You might discover a topic that really interests you and that you want to pursue beyond the research for a specific article. Is there a book there? Maybe. Add this to your idea folder.

There are many opportunities for writers in the business world. Many of these have helped freelancers (including me) build a sustainable business.

Marketing Collateral
Collateral covers a wide range of types of projects and it refers to brochures and other material that a company uses to support its marketing efforts. Some, such as brochures, may be one-time projects, others, such as newsletters, fit well into a monthly marketing retainer. Styles will vary from piece to piece and client to client but generally speaking, you can expect advertising and marketing material to be less formal than other types of writing. Having said that, informality is not an excuse for

bad or incorrect writing. The goal is to sell, so be persuasive and try to connect with your audience.

Advertising
Good advertising copy is a result of experience and skill. Pay attention to sales letters, magazine ads, direct mail and print ads to get a feel for the style and how it differs from articles and other types of collateral. There is very limited space in advertising so the key is to make every word count. Headlines need to be benefit driven and grab a reader's attention. Stress the benefits of the product or service you are promoting and make sure these benefits are relevant to your audience. Endorsements are good. The word FREE is better when trying to get a prospect to "pay attention."

There are many good books on writing advertising copy (see Resources) and this is not the place for a course in the subject. It's a specialized kind of writing and if you have not done it before, consider signing up for a class at a local college or university. You'll get some experience and maybe a few samples for your portfolio. Visuals need to support the copy and vice versa so you will likely need to work with a graphic designer.

Conference Highlights
If your clients attend conferences, make sure you check in with the client when they return. Even better, meet with them before they leave so they know what to think about in terms of future content. If the conference was

successful, they will come back with new ideas to either write about or on which they can comment. If they had a speaking position, even better. Offer to take their presentation or notes and turn it into an article. They've already done most of the work and if their topic was accepted at a conference, it is likely to be of interest to others in the industry.

White papers
White papers provide thought leadership, expertise or a position on specific topics, and typically run from about four to about 20 pages. While educational in nature, companies often use them as promotional pieces (usually business-to-business companies versus companies that sell directly to consumers). The best walk a fine line between information, research and promotion.

Brochures
Unlike white papers, the goal here is to be promotional. How you approach this, however, will depend on the industry. A product brochure for a piece of industrial equipment is going to be technical – while still promoting the positive. On the other hand, it's hard to imagine being too "flowery" if you are writing for a bridal store. A good writer is flexible.

Direct Response also know as Direct Marketing Copywriting
Direct response is everywhere. It includes letters and advertisements you get in the mail, marketing emails to

potential customers, and text on brochures, billboards and broadcast media. Why is there so much? Because it works.

The difference between direct response content and more general marketing and advertising material is that the goal of direct response material is to get a response in the form of a sale or an inquiry, by phone, mail or an on-line inquiry or order.

There are many books on direct response copywriting. So, if you're interested (and it does pay well) pick up a book or two and read them. *American Writers & Artists* (awaionline.com), for instance, offers "The Accelerated Program for Six-Figure Copywriting." Read your mail – yes the "junk" mail. Watch cable television (gym equipment ads are a good example) and look at ads

Testing in Direct Response

Direct response marketing campaigns are built on testing and it is important to understand this process before you start writing. Let's say a company is selling financial services. They will test formats, content, lists, graphics and more. Not all at once of course, but it is an ongoing process. If you can produce a "winner," you'll get asked to do more, that's great. But pretty soon, it will be put up against another competitor. Testing is a constant in direct response and is based on math. How much did the program cost, how many responses were received and what was the cost per response or per sale?

in magazines and newspapers. The common link is that there is a call to action.

You can do the math but the point is that, no matter how well written you think your work was, direct marketing efforts are judged strictly by results. So while awards are nice, a direct response campaign that doesn't make money is judged a failure.

Writing for the Web
Every business has a website. Yet most of these sites do not get nearly the attention they need. Generally, it's because a business doesn't have the staff or expertise to do a good job keeping it current or optimizing it for search engines. Thus it's a rapidly growing area as more and more people turn to the web for purchasing information. (Remember, your first sample is your own website!)

Writing website copy is a necessary part of your tool kit if you want to write marketing copy. Most companies, especially small to mid-sized companies, don't want to have to hire different freelancers for brochures and websites. Freelancers must be able to diversify their skills, despite inevitable learning curves. Remember, time is money for you and your client.

Email Marketing
Today, many companies rely on email to get sales and inquiries. These campaigns are often comprised of a

series of emails, sent out periodically, intended to encourage readers to buy or request additional information. The subject line of the email is often just as important as the actual content. This often determines, after all, whether the reader will even open it. Spend the time you need to make it good. Then make sure the content of the email lives up to the promise in the subject line.

Newsletters

Newsletters are a cash cow for many freelancers, whether online or in print. When used for external communications (i.e. customers and prospects), they can include anything from new product introductions, new personnel introductions and, case studies. Bigger companies may have an internal newsletter that goes to employees. The tone will be more familiar than in an external newsletter but content often overlaps. There is always something to write about and, as an added benefit to writers, newsletters are (or should be) sent on a regular basis, thus providing regular income.

e-newsletters

These are often an electronic form of the traditional print newsletter and have advantages over their hard copy cousin. First, they're a lot cheaper to distribute. Second, there is no space limitation although short intros with links to full articles work best. Plus, templates such as Constant Contact can help you individualize the template, add graphics and more to visually enhance the newsletter. These additions can be very expensive to use in a print edition.

If you're really ambitious, having a good grasp of available and relevant lists will be helpful to your client who is likely to appreciate your initiative.

Executive Bios

If a company has a website, they need biographies. Since people come and go, this can turn into a fairly regular source of income. Pricing is a little tough here because some people will already have bios and all you may need is to change the format. Other times you will have to interview the person, write, then edit. My suggestion? Charge by the hour, or by the bio, assuming that the time will even out.

Advertorials

Advertorials are promotional "articles." But unlike editorial content, the company pays for the space – just like advertising and, like advertising, you are allowed to (and expected to) say how wonderful the company/CEO/product is. Be judicious in your use of superlatives! Too many and you lose the credibility that advertorials are supposed to elicit. They are meant to look like an article in a magazine but are usually labeled advertorials to indicate to readers that this is not editorial content.

Case Studies
Case studies have been a staple of marketing collateral for a long time. Typically, they run two to five pages, so they're not long and that usually includes graphics (charts, pictures, etc.). Businesses use case studies to tell prospective customers about the successful experiences they have had. They can be used in a marketing portfolio, in a mailing or, frequently, on a website.

While some companies may use their own format, the essence of a case study is straightforward:

1. The background on the business for whom they have done the work;
2. The challenge (or problem);
3. The solution or how your client was able to solve a problem for their customer
4. The results. Be as specific as possible. Some companies are understandably reluctant to give out information especially financial results. Expressing results in a percentage format (e.g. an increase of 10%) rather than dollars can alleviate this concern.

Content Marketing
From the Content Marketing Institute:
"Content marketing is a strategic marketing approach focused on creating and distributing valuable, relevant, and consistent content to attract and retain a clearly-defined audience — and, ultimately, to drive profitable customer action."

Content marketing is gaining in importance as companies learn to develop more sustainable customer relationships. While it easily overlaps with articles, brochures, etc., the purpose is generally more educational and the style less promotional.

Conferences and Speaking
Just as you can find multiple publications dedicated to almost any industry or topic, so too can you find a conference that is relevant for almost any client. In fact helping your business clients find speaking engagements is a great way to add value. This involves researching relevant conferences, finding out as much as you can about attendees and costs, and learning their policy regarding speakers. Most conferences will have a formal speaker proposal. Others will just ask for a description of the session and bios of the speakers.

Conferences are also a great way to get double duty from your work. Maybe you've already published an article that is relevant to the conference theme and you can repurpose the topic and research and turn it into a speaker proposal. Alternatively, if you get a speaking slot for a client you may be able to repurpose that into an article. Either way, it's a win-win.

One note of caution. More and more conferences are conducted on a "pay to play" model. That is, if a company sponsors a conference they are either more likely to, or even guaranteed, a slot on the agenda. The model clearly has its flaws, but make sure you know the lay of the land before you hand in a report.

Annual Reports
You don't have to be a financial person to write an annual report. The financial people will give you the data, charts and graphs you need. But you will need to supply content that speaks to the company's activities during the past year and future goals in a professional way. This will require extensive interviews with corporate executives, probably in different areas of management including operations, product development, marketing, etc. Take a good look at previous annual reports – they can often provide a rough template and an idea of tone.

Annual reports are not easy, especially if you don't have a business background, but they usually pay well.

Public Relations
Public relations is a broad category that involves a business's efforts to get their name out in the media. The hope is that when a customer or prospect sees the article, they will either call the company or it will, at least, add to the company's name recognition and credibility. Does it work? Yes. Can you prove it? That's tougher. The phone doesn't ring the minute an article appears. It can take time, but when done well, a public relations campaign can build credibility, recognition, and sales for most companies.

Note: Some people measure results by the space used. That is, if an article is a full page, it is compared to how much a full-page ad would cost. I'm not sure that does the article justice in terms of its value.

Many companies enjoy, and their business benefits from, the publicity that having an article under their byline can bring. Few companies, however, have the staff with the time to pitch these articles and get them done. This is a great opportunity. You don't even have to be an expert in a specific topic or business. You do, however, have to be a good interviewer, researcher and editor.

A word of caution: Companies often think that the more promotional and the more they can get in about how wonderful the company/CEO/product is, the better. They're usually wrong and will often get an article rejected. Save the promotion for the brochures. Magazines want content that will help/entertain/interest their readers. Your client will benefit by having their byline, and maybe a short biography, on an article and the credibility that comes with it.

Writing for Advertising and Public Relations Agencies
Advertising and public relations agencies often hire freelancers as a back-up resource and a good relationship with a busy firm can help to ensure a steady income.

Content Mills

According to Wikipedia, a content farm (or content mill) is a company that employs large numbers of freelance writers to generate large amounts of textual content which is specifically designed to satisfy algorithms for maximal retrieval by automated search engines. Their main goal is to generate advertising revenue through attracting reader page views, as first exposed in the context of social spam."

What's that mean? Basically that these content farms provide inexpensive content to their clients that can be put on the Internet to increase traffic and increase search engine optimization (SEO). Writing for content mills can take the form of articles, blogs, posts – there's a wide range.

Content mills are often looked down upon by freelancers. They pay badly, often have impossible deadlines, and typically don't allow writers to be creative. You could be writing about headaches and mortgage insurance in the same day. You have to research quickly and accurately, and write even faster all for what often comes down to a penny or two (sometimes three or four cents) a word.

Many people think content mills take advantage of writers. In some cases, it's probably true. But it's an option to consider – especially at the beginning of your freelancing career. Is it worth it? If you're new to freelancing look at is as boot camp, where you can get some experience. In the end though, you're unlikely to make a living at it.

These relationships can take many forms. An agency may want you to appear to the client as if you are an employee or you may be required to stay entirely in the background, having contact with the agency only. Occasionally, you may be brought in to meet the client and interact directly. I've done all three and, if I had to pick, I'd say my preference was working directly with the agency. Agencies need to make money. So they will often ask you for a discounted rate so they can mark up your services. That's your call.

One of the things I really like about working with bigger agencies is that they often develop "creative briefs" which they will share. These documents are an overall look at the strategy, goals, media and other components of a comprehensive marketing strategy. You'll just be a small part of that but it will give you a perspective and a view that will help you become an integral part of the team.

Editing
Freelance editing jobs are another option to consider. There are three types of editing – copy, line and developmental - and there is a later chapter devoted to just this. For now, it is important to know that this opportunity exists and can generate good income.

Grant Writing
Let's say a local charity that helps foster children wants to raise money. A grant writer would write a proposal to be sent to the appropriate government or foundation that

donates to similar causes. Grant writers also often help to find the relevant grantors.

Grant writing is a very specific skill. Read a book on grant writing. Take a class at a local college or university. The most basic grant applications will ask about the organization, its management and most importantly, require a strong statement as to why the organization is deserving of their limited funds. Others, especially those that offer large amounts of money and/or those that are based on science, can get much more complicated. It is your job to work with your client to ensure that the statement is compelling. Remember, funding is always competitive and your understanding of how the process works will be as important as understanding your client and their mission.

The other part of grant writing is knowing what grants may be available and appropriate for your non-profit client. The art is in finding a good match. In fact, that may be the key to setting you apart from other grant writers. To start, take a good look at www.foundationcenter.org. Not only is there good information but there is also an accessible database of more than 5,000 funding sources – with subject listings.

Blogs
This is a kind of amorphous topic. Some people think a blog post is a 200-300 word piece with a very targeted opinion or direction. Others post "blogs" that are 1000

words or more and include interviews and more. The problem is, those that post these types of "blogs" tend to pay what they think a "blog" is worth versus and article. The good news is that blog posts can be a great way to gain entry into a company's communications strategy leading to bigger projects, or they can be a great way to generate repeat income. But take care to make sure that you and your client are on the same page when it comes to the scope of the work and payment terms.

Catalogs

Take a look at *The J. Peterman Company* catalog for what I consider to be the gold standard. If you have a favorite catalog and have some familiarity with their offerings, pick a few products and try your hand at it. If you like it and you think you have some talent, consider sending a query with these samples to the catalog company.

Specialized Content

Just as you can develop a niche for articles, you can also develop an industry niche for marketing material. For instance, a real estate broker who wants to break into freelancing might consider creating ads, flyers and online descriptions.

Speeches

Most people, from politicians to corporate executives, don't write their own speeches. Speechwriters can demand significant sums and freelancers can make money here. But, and this is a big but, if you haven't crafted speeches before, take a class, read a book, do something that will help educate you in the process. Try writing a speech, about anything, and read it aloud. What do you think? Try it before a couple of friends and take their comments seriously. It also helps to get to know the person who will be speaking. Style is important. For instance, some people are comfortable with jokes. Others are not.

Often you can take a speech and pitch it to a magazine in the same industry space with a good chance of it being accepted. If the speech is before an organization, that group may have its own publication and be very happy to print the article. So, with some changes, you might be able to add another article to your portfolio.

Resume Writing
It's not romantic and while you may not be able to charge more than $150 or so (depending on where you are), once you get known in your area as a resume writer, it can be profitable. After you do a few, a basic resume probably won't take you more than two hours – including an interview with the individual if needed. A more complicated one will take longer but the charge should be commensurate with your time.

Chapter 2
Generating Ideas for Publications

Some of your work for publications is likely to be "on assignment." That is, they determine the article topic. That's great but waiting for them to contact you is not great. You need to be proactive in developing and pursuing salable topics. In fact, that's probably going to be the difference between mediocre success and financial freedom.

"They" (you know, the universal "they") say to write what you know. It's not bad advice, especially if there is an area in which you have significant experience and expertise. But in a world of Google and Siri, there's really not much you can't find out. So don't let a lack of knowledge in a particular area limit you. That doesn't mean that you should start out with a topic that's entirely new – that's going to be really tough to pitch. It does mean that if you're not an expert already don't worry; there are plenty of sources to tap (more on that in Chapter 4).

New Ideas
Always have a notepad with you – whether it's an app on your phone or tablet, or an actual pen and paper. (I have been known to use a napkin and I am not alone). You never know when an idea will strike. Keep something near your bed, so you're ready when ideas appear just as you are falling asleep. Keep paper and/or electronic files

of all these ideas. Not all of these ideas are going to be good ones and over time you are likely to toss more than you keep. You just never know – and you don't want to forget a good idea.

Use your background to delve more deeply into topics that might not be covered by others with less knowledge. Did you work as a high school guidance counselor? Are there tips on getting into college that you might be able to uniquely offer? Did you start a new business? Would other prospective entrepreneurs be able to learn from your experience?

I have a friend who is a professional photographer. She sees the world differently than I do. She sees fantastic photos where I just see a backdrop. This is, as a freelancer, the kind of skill you need to develop from a content point of view.

Try these:

- Read blogs and articles in areas of interest. Using a good idea as a takeoff point doesn't mean you are plagiarizing or copying another's ideas. Writers often inspire other writers. Contribute to blogs and comment on articles if you see an opportunity. You never know what a response will trigger.
- Review editorial calendars to see areas of focus coming up.

- Keep holidays in mind. Publications always need content for these special issues but be sure to pitch these articles at least three months ahead.
- Watch the news and, where possible, tie your ideas to a timely topic.
- Ask people! Sounds simple and it is. If you and a friend are interested in a particular topic, say sports, ask them what questions they might like answered.
- Try a change of scenery. It can recharge your brain!
- Go back over your ideas periodically. Recent information can help you put a new spin on an old idea.
- Join a local writer's association. It's motivating and you'll be exposed to different types of writing and new outlets.

Writing About People, For People

People like reading about people. Period. Your subject doesn't need to be a celebrity, an inventor or the oldest, wisest, fastest, or best at anything. Rather, they have to have an interesting story. I have a friend who knew a man who had worked as a doorman at the Plaza Hotel in New York for decades. One can only imagine what he has seen and heard in his career. This could be a great human-interest story for a travel magazine. A large, national consumer publication might not be interested in how a local teacher made a difference but local publications and teaching magazines will.

Curiosity Is Key

Not writing for the national media yet? That's okay. It can still be a great source for local stories. Is immigration a timely issue? Do you have an immigrant family near you with a story to tell? How about roadwork and infrastructure? Is there a local engineering firm with a story to tell? Topics around a sustainable environment are not likely to go away anytime soon. Do you have a nearby college or university with an expert on sustainable agriculture? How about a company that sells solar panels? They'd be happy to tell you about the growth of their business. They may even tell you about some of the challenges they have faced. Similarly, there may be something really exciting happening in your neighborhood that could form the basis for a larger story.

Writing for Organizations

Some people call me crazy but I love working with professional firms. Especially accountants and lawyers. Why? Because they all seem to have lots to say. Take a medium-sized law firm, with multiple departments. Each department (depending on the size of the firm these can include real estate, intellectual property, estates, business, international law, finance, and more) will have its own target audience with specific target publications. And there will be topics galore for each. I usually start by sitting down with whoever is managing the communications effort and schedule (in person or on the phone) meetings with as many professionals as I can.

Ask these individuals what the "hot topics" are in their area. Are there new regulations? Are there trends on which they would like to comment? What are their clients asking them? These will get them to start talking. You will have more than enough for at least a few articles. Plus, most will already have published an article or two and maybe even presented at multiple conferences. Most of these topics can be repurposed. The downside to working with professionals is that you are usually relegated to the "non-billable" pile. Their clients have to come first. Try to make it as easy as possible for them.

Just as professional firms have departments, most businesses will have their own divisions that can add fodder to your ideas. Take a manufacturer, for example. There is the marketing department of course, but there are also product development people who would be happy to tell you about the latest and greatest features of their product. Read the magazines that are important to them to make sure you have an idea as to what is already out there being discussed. Perhaps there is a discussion in which your client can participate.

How about an industry association? Here too there are many roads to publication. Maybe the association will foot the bill to promote members. If so, you have just increased your billable pile exponentially. Does the association hold conferences? Will publicity expand their reach?

Ideas Are Cheap But Good Ones Are Invaluable
A successful freelancer will have hundreds, if not thousands, of ideas over the course of their career. Some will sell, others won't. That's okay. Train your mind to be open to new thoughts and new ideas. You'll be surprised how many ideas you will have. Over time, you'll get better at developing ideas and learning which ones will work.

Chapter 3
Query Letters: Asking for the Assignment

A "query letter," sometimes known as a "pitch" letter, is a letter to an editor that describes the topic you want to write about, why their readers would be interested, and why you are the right person to write it. It is where you ask the editor to place their confidence in you, your idea, and your research to create an article that will be of interest and of value to their readers. And to pay you for your efforts. The ability to draft a successful query forms the foundation for a successful freelancing career. So take it very seriously.

Selecting Your Targets
There is almost always going to be more than one, sometimes many more, publications that may have an interest in your query. Check multiple sources to make sure you have the universe well covered. Google the topic you want to pitch and see where other articles have been published. Then check out those publications. It is likely that at least one or two will be a new potential outlet for your article.

Which brings up the questions, should you pitch to multiple magazines at the same time? That's tricky. Editors, understandably, don't want to see the same article in another magazine, especially one with a competitive readership. Makes sense! One way to handle this is to pitch your first choice (maybe the one that pays the best or offers the best audience for your client). While a lack of response (either yay or nay) may seem rude, it typically means the editor is not interested. But things do happen and things do get lost. If you don't hear from them in a couple of weeks, follow up, politely. If the topic is time-sensitive, you will need to follow up sooner. If you still don't get a response (or if the response is negative) feel free to continue down your list.

To increase your chances, before you pitch:

- Read at least two or three issues of the publication. Get an idea of the style used and what the publication covers. How long is the typical article? Are there specific departments that might accept your work? For instance, new products, people, or management. It's tough to recover if you've sent an irrelevant query.
- Read the media kit. It will tell you about the demographics of their readership. This is a key piece of information when explaining why your topic will attract their readers.
- Look at the advertisers. This can be helpful when trying to understand their readers. Are the ads targeted to women? Teens? Hobbyists? Men? Homeowners? Are the ads for high-end luxury items?
- Look at the writing style. Do they use first person articles? Are they informational? Literary? Educational? Newsy? Do they use how-to articles?

- Use many different iterations in your search (e.g. sailing, sail boats) to ensure that your topic hasn't been recently covered or how you may be able to change the angle to make it different.
- Google your topic. The results are often surprising (even if the publication you are pitching hasn't done a similar article in a while, they are not likely to be excited about a story topic that has recently been run by a competitor). If there is nothing or very little about your topic, take a moment to consider why. Is it so esoteric that few people might be interested? If there is a lot, that's good news in terms of your research opportunities but may not bode well for acceptance of another article especially in a limited market.
- Make sure you know the name of the editor to whom you are writing. By the way, email is fine but don't call unless you can't get through otherwise or you already have an established relationship with the editor.

Editorial Calendars

Editorial calendars are a great place to look to find a home for your article. They are generally part of a publication's media kit (these contain information used by advertisers) and will list the editorial focus of upcoming issues. For instance, if you are working for an insurance client, look at a publication like *LifeHealth Pro*, *Life & Health Advisor* or *Best's Review*. You will see monthly themes that include health insurance, baby boomers, technology and innovative industry products and you can plan your pitch accordingly. If your client is a clothing retailer, you are likely to find fashion themes in many consumer publications. With this information, you can add something relevant to your query, such as "I noticed that your March issue features marketing to Baby Boomers. The proposed article will cover the use of database marketing and specifically address the Boomer market."

Construction of the Query

There are usually five parts to a query and you have a lot of ground to cover but it's best to keep it down to a max of 1½ pages. Shorter is better. If the editor likes the idea and needs more information, they'll ask. Your letter will include:

- A personal salutation;
- A strong lead and introduction to the topic;
- Author introduction;
- Business details; and
- Close.

Salutation

While it can be a benefit to have a track record with an editor, it isn't possible, for even the most published writer, to know everyone. That is not an excuse for you to fall back on the "Dear Sir or Madam/Editor" format. Find out the editor's name. How? Check the masthead in the publication (it's probably online) or check the website under editorial staff. If that doesn't work, call and ask. "Dear Sir or Madam" shows a lack of initiative and energy.

Which brings up another question and that is, to whom should you address the query? While it may be tempting to go right to the top of the masthead (usually the publisher), that's not usually the right place to start. For most publications, probably the best place to start is the Managing Editor. They are often more hands-on than an editor-in-chief or publisher and even if they're not the right person, they will probably forward it appropriately. If you're pitching to bigger publications, with specific department/column editors, try them first. They may even have a submissions editor though these people are often interns whose job it is to whittle down the slush pile (what used to be a physical pile and is now more likely to be an email mailbox that is a collection of unsolicited queries and submissions). This is not really where you want to be.

Lead and Topic Intro
Start with a strong lead. The goal is to grab the editor's attention, just as you want the article to grab the reader's attention. I often end up using the first sentence of my query as the lead to the article.

The best way to ensure a solid query is to do some initial research. For instance, if you are pitching an article on the restaurant scene in Philadelphia, a statistic on the growth of the industry in the area would strengthen your case. A quote from a local restaurateur would probably be even better.

Author Introduction

If you're writing the article for a client, it is likely that they will want their own byline. That's okay. You get paid to write the article, not to have your name on it, unless that's part of the deal. Writing articles for others, under their name, can be very lucrative. Placement is much easier when the author (not the writer) is a recognized expert.

If you're writing your own article, and you're already a recognized expert in your field, great! If not, getting an assignment can be a challenge, but it's far from insurmountable. If you have clips, include a few to show the strength of your writing, not necessarily your knowledge of the subject matter. If you plan to interview others (and they have said yes!), explain who your sources will be. Interviews with experts are always good, but make sure you can deliver on these promises.

Business Details

If you've done your homework, you should have an idea as to the style, approximate length and other details that are consistent in the publication. Show you've done your due diligence with a sentence like "The article will be approximately xxxx words (base this on the writer's guidelines) and I would be able to provide photos of (the subject, author, product, etc.).

Close
I have attached a few clips for your review (or other supporting material). Thank you for your consideration and I look forward to working with you.

Sincerely,
Name
Phone
Email

Sample query 1

The client is a direct marketing/data analytics company serving specific vertical industries including marketing agencies. This query was successfully submitted to direct marketing publications whose audience includes the company's prospective clients. Target publications included Direct Marketing News, Target Marketing, ChiefMarketer and others.

Dear John; *(personal salutation: I use Mr./Ms. the first time I have contact with them)*

(lead) It's tempting to use state-of-the-art marketing technology to communicate with prospects and customers in real-time. According to research marketers and agencies perceive the top three benefits of real-time marketing to be: a better customer experience, improved conversion rates, and improved customer retention.

At the same time, real-time presents real challenges, including appropriately personalizing messages based on consumer behavior and the possibility of consumer overload. *(This lead sets up the paragraph and I would probably use something close to it for the lead in the article.)*

Real-time marketing can work. But not every situation calls for an instant marketing message or offer. We live in an age where consumers are in control. They demand communications at a time when it is most suitable to their needs, through the channels they prefer. The concept of "marketing in the moment" is evolving into the idea of marketing at the right moment.

To meet this demand for "right time, right channel messaging," marketers must use up-to-date data such as: where consumers have been, what they are doing, who they are, and which channels they use. It's the 4 Rs: the Right Person, the Right Channel, the Right Moment, and the Right Answer.

(business details) I propose an article titled "The Move From Real-Time to Right-Time Marketing" that, utilizing case studies, would explain this evolution and address exactly what Right-Time marketing means to businesses.

The article would be bylined by _____*name and title and Company Name if relevant. Add a sentence about the author's credentials and, if relevant, about the company.*

Be careful not to appear promotional. For instance, it's okay to say xyz company is a leader in its industry but do not say providing the best in ....)

(Close) Thank you for your consideration and we are looking forward to working with you.

Sample Query 2

The client is a major horse show that attracts competitors from around the world. Their goal is to increase their exposure in the equine community and attract more competitors and spectators. Fund-raising is a sub-text here as well.

Potential target publications include most equestrian publications (a few aren't relevant to this type of equestrian activity) as well as regional consumer publications (online and offline) that will reach people looking for a fun activity.

Here's an example where I would submit simultaneous queries (though press releases would go to all). The following query focuses on a specific competitor who is from the area where the show is located.

Dear (editor's name):

(Name) has been riding horses, literally, since before she was born. Her mother (name) was a dressage competitor and her dad (name) is a trainer. They work together at (farm name and location) and have built a business that is well-known and respected for their horses, their riding and their training.

(name) has been competing since she was 5 years old, showing in the Juniors and moving up through Grand Prix levels. (for consumer publications I changed this language to – showing in junior levels and moving up to professional classes). She is also very active supporter in the sport, is a Board member for the (association) and works actively to encourage youth to participate in the sport.

I would like to propose a profile on (name). The article would talk about her early interest in riding, her move up through the competitive ranks, and what her future goals are for herself, the farm, and the sport itself.

for regional publications – (name) will be showing at (name of horse show) this fall. We would include a brief description of (the show), what it has to offer, and provide logistical details for those who might want to attend and can provide additional photos of the show.

We would supply photos – of her early years as well as current photos including, of course, her horses. Her comments will be an important part of the article.

Thank you for your consideration.

Ginny Simon
Phone
Email

This topic obviously holds interest for equestrian publications (there is even one that publishes exclusively profiles) but in addition, local publications love to do features on local people. In this case too, I was able to reach out to different regional newspapers and magazines with non-competitive circulations. This is an interesting example in that it has interest to both business-to-business publications (equestrian publications targeted to industry participants) and consumer publications that always like local "celebrities." Post-show publicity is possible too, especially if she wins!

Following Up
I have heard some people (including editors) say that follow-ups are not a good idea. I respectfully disagree on the condition that your follow-up is polite, that you adhere to the preferences they suggested in their guidelines or in *Writer's Market* and that you don't follow up more than once.

The follow-up should be concise. For instance:

"I am writing to follow-up on my query dated _____, suggesting an article titled _____." If you have, in

the interim, uncovered a new point of interest or a new source, mention that as well.

I use email to follow-up and try to avoid calling. However, if there is time sensitivity or the elapsed time has gone beyond their deadlines, go ahead and call. If you get voice mail, leave a message. And if they don't call back, let it go and try another publication. You may have to go back and tweak the query to better fit the next publication, but it's worth doing.

Never assume you know the audience better than the editor. Phrases like "your readers will love/appreciate/buy your magazine because of" will turn most editors off.

Sometimes, an editor will be interested in your topic but not have a place for it. So they file it. In the meantime, you have moved on and begun work on an assignment from

Note: Writers are often fearful that editors will "steal" their idea. I have published hundreds of articles and have never had that happen. What has happened is that the editor already had a similar article in the works. It happens. Period. Move on. And if you're really suspicious, just don't query that editor again.

your second choice. Then you get a call from the first editor. Don't burn bridges. Explain to the first editor what happened. They will understand. Think of it like a prom, go with the one that said yes first. Editors move from publication to publication – often.

Be Ready for Rejection
Finally, be ready for rejection letters. Everyone gets them – lots of them. They don't necessarily mean that your idea was bad. Maybe there is already an article in the works on the same topic. Maybe your query just did not capture the editor's imagination. Unless you know the editor well, you many never find out. Fact is that publications get lots of queries and a rejection may simply be because they are scheduled too far out.

Rejection letters can be useful tools to any writer if they provide insight into why the article was rejected. Form letters are, however, too often the norm. At least they close the door and let you go on to pitch elsewhere.

Writing on Spec
Writing on spec is writing on assignment but without the promise of payment. In some cases, you may do it for free. Or the publication may "pay on acceptance," that is, if they accept the article, you get paid. In either case, it can be a worthwhile endeavor, adding to your portfolio, building a relationship with an editor and practicing your craft. Best case? You write an article on spec for a publication in which you are truly interested, they accept

it, they pay for it, and they give you another assignment. Worst case? You gain experience.

Chapter 4
Look It Up! Researching Your Article

While it's always nice (and often profitable) to have a specific area of expertise, most assignments depend on the writer's ability to get the information they need in a timely manner.

Years ago, I wrote for a local business publication. It was a monthly and I wrote on topics ranging from landscaping to business insurance. Was I an expert on any of these topics? Not by a long shot. But I did my research. First, I looked up articles on the same topic, read them and took notes. Then I talked to people in each of the businesses. If their opinions did not agree, I kept going until I was sure the information was accurate. Finally, I wrote the article. These were not technical or scientific articles. They were overviews of specific areas of business and my research allowed me to garner the information I needed to write an accurate and helpful article.

However, even if you consider yourself well-versed in an area, good research adds credibility to you as an author and to your article. Plus it will inspire confidence on the part of the editor and give you a competitive advantage over other writers who don't go the extra mile. So, unless you are a recognized expert, don't skip this important step.

Even fiction writers benefit from research—whether it is historic, social or scientific—by offering a context for their story.

You must cite your sources, accurately and in the format dictated by the assignment. Be careful of statements like "Experts agree..." You may decide to distill information from multiple experts into a more general comment for a non-scientific publication but many people agree even for a more informal article, be ready to support your statement for editors or readers who may have questions.

Primary Sources v. Secondary Sources
The words, "hard" and "soft" research have different criteria and expectations. Hard research includes scientific and objective research; that is, information that can be clearly documented by facts, figures, statistics and evidence. Soft research covers topics that are more subjective, cultural and opinion-based and, as such, are subject to less scrutiny.

From *Wikipedia*: "Secondary research (also known as desk research) involves the summary, collation and/or synthesis of existing research rather than primary research in which data are collected from, for example, research subjects or experiments." Depending on the publication or the goal of the assignment, secondary sources may be sufficient.

Primary sources include (but are not limited to):
- Original, firsthand accounts of an event or time period (diaries, letters, journals, newspapers);
- Original reports of scientific discoveries;
- Results of experiments; or
- Interviews with someone who has firsthand knowledge of your subject (e.g. a scientist conducting an experiment).

Secondary sources include (but are not limited to):
- Biographies;
- Histories;
- Analysis of a clinical trial;
- Newspaper or magazine articles that interpret; or
- Individuals who have knowledge of or about the subject.

Where to Look

As mentioned, technology makes some research easy. I like to start with *Wikipedia* but note the word "start" – it's important. *Wikipedia* is great for an overall view but, other than using it for definitions, most do not consider it a credible source, especially on its own. Use it for background and for a starting point for more research.

Then try Google or another search engine. The most likely problem here is that you will be faced with thousands if not millions of hits. For instance, if you're doing an article for a parenting magazine on children and sailing, I would

Google sailing, sailing with children, and water sports and children, and children and boats. (I did and got a total of about 100,000,000 results.) Obviously you can't read them all, nor do you want to, but do a quick overview of the first 5-10 pages to determine which sources make sense. (Note: If you are writing an article on an issue or topic that has conflicting opinions, it is important to make sure that you use sources from different sides of the issue.)

Through this review, you may also be able to identify people who you think would be able to provide valuable insight and data for the article.

PR People
First, a disclaimer. Most of my work is PR, so I have an affinity for the trade. I love it when writers call.

PR people have an agenda – one that can help you do your job better. Their job is to work with the media and writers to get them the information they need. So, if you need product information, try the PR department. If you want to set up an interview with a corporate executive, start with the PR department. If you want to interview a celebrity, their publicist (or PR person) is the one who can help. If you are doing a travel piece and you need to get information on venues, contact the PR department. That's their job.

Associations

Looking for travel statistics? Try the US Travel Association or the Travel & Tourism Research Association. International travel? Try the Global Business Travel Association. How about something a little more adventurous? Contact The Adventure Travel Trade Association. Or The Africa Travel Association.

How about an article on orchids? The American Orchid Society has more than 500 affiliated societies that have local groups with members who would be happy to provide information for an article. Insurance? There are many – some focused on marketing, others on administration – it is a long list. Most have their own publications that accept articles.

There is an association (and publication) for almost any subject you can think of – just Google it and add the word "association." Even better, these people are happy to talk about their industry.

On a similar note, consider contacting consulting firms in your field of interest – especially for business articles. While they are not likely to provide detailed information that their clients pay for, they may be willing to help in order to get their name out.

Government

Federal and state governments have huge depositories of data and statistics that can help you add credibility (there's that word again) to your article. Writing about farming and want to know the biggest crop in Arkansas? Try the Arkansas State Department of Agriculture. I know getting through to people can be a challenge but once you do, they can be a great resource.

Local government offices are great sources as well. Your representatives and senators, on both a state and federal level, often have a staff of interns whose job it is to help their constituents (i.e. voters).

Libraries
You know libraries. Those buildings that are home to thousands of books, computers, research material and, most importantly, librarians. Their job has changed dramatically over the past years but only in technique. Most are ready, willing and able to help you get the information you need and it's free. Don't forget college and university libraries although there may be some restrictions on assisting non-students.

The Research Process
Make sure to keep your notes. I've had articles published and later, even months later, readers have a question. I keep my notes with detailed sourcing and am able to pass on this information. It's important. Whether you file your information on paper, on your computer or both, make sure the information is accessible.

Taking notes and keeping records is part of your job as a writer. Whether you use 3x5 index cards, a reporter's notebook, a tablet or a phone, find the method(s) that works best for you. You never know when questions might arise or when you might need to go back to the source for another article.

Evaluating Your Sources
Following the 2016 election, one of the many topics addressed by the administration and the media was misinformation that was circulated on social media – even traditional media. Some of this was from individuals, some was from false "news" sources and, the consensus seems to be, that it happened on both sides. Bottom line? Be really, really careful. Misinformation goes far beyond politics and ranges from simple mistakes to deliberate errors and, with the click of a button, this misinformation can reach millions instantly.

Confirm your sources. My rule of thumb is that if I have three credible sources that agree, it's probably okay. The standards for investigative reporting and contentious topics are higher. Of course, when you are doing medical or scientific work, the research must be more hardcore.

Medical and scientific research needs to be published in a credible publication or database to be of ultimate value. Credible sources can be in the form of articles in medical journals (try Medline.com) in well-respected medical magazines such as *Scientific American*, or on well-researched websites such as WebMD.com. You can increase the credibility of these sources by assuring they are written by well-respected authorities.

Here are some questions you should ask yourself about every source you use:

- Is the source current? Depending on your topic, the definition of "current" may vary.
- Who is the intended audience?
- Who is the author and what are his or her credentials?
- Has any of the information been reviewed? For instance, is it a peer-reviewed journal?
- Can you verify the information from personal knowledge or another source?
- Does the sponsoring organization have an agenda or bias? If so, it does not mean that you can't use the information, just that you need to clearly identify your source.

It can be okay to use "as quoted in" but make sure both the original source and the secondary source are credible. I usually Google the quote to verify it.

Then there is the CRAAP test: (adapted by Sara Memmott, Social Work Librarian, Eastern Michigan University, from the Meriam Library at California State University Chico)

- **C**urrency – When was the information published and has it been revised or updated. Are links current?
- **R**elevance – Does the information relate to your topic? Is it an appropriate level for your audience?
- **A**uthority – Is the source credible? What are the author's credentials or affiliations?
- **A**ccuracy – Is the information truthful, reliable and correct? Can you verify the information?
- **P**urpose – Is the intent to inform, teach, or persuade and are the author's intentions clear?

When Do You Start – and Stop?
Research begins as soon as you decide on a topic. Most people start with a general search, gradually narrowing down the sources and information. Questions will usually begin to arise as you work on the article so keep your sources handy.

It's pretty easy to get bogged down in research. Whether you are getting paid $100 or $1,000, you want to maintain a minimum hourly rate. So you have to stop at some point. Where that point is depends on the topic and the amount of information you are compiling. If you have any concerns about the information you have received, verify it until you are comfortable.

Look at the article from the reader's point of view. Does it provide useful and accurate information appropriate to the publication and the target audience? Is there anything the editor or reader will question? No article answers every question and good articles often raise questions, but these questions should not be about your research.

Additional Sources

- Scholarly research or peer reviewed journals (these can be expensive but access is on the rise. Don't forget librarians are your friends.)
- Edited or authored books
- First person accounts
- Interviews (more about this in Chapter 5)
- Case studies
- Surveys
- Specialized areas, such as legal research, will have their own preferred sources
- White papers from companies
- Legal and governmental information

Images

Just as most industry publications no longer pay for articles, they may not pay for a photographer either. It can be very helpful to them – and an added incentive to getting your article published – if you do some image research on your own. Companies may have their own photo library. Google Images offers thousands but there are costs and you need to be careful that they are not cost-prohibitive and that you have the appropriate permission and credit.

Chapter 5
Interviewing

Most of the articles you write will require interviews. They lend experience, knowledge, and credibility to your article and good interviews can set you apart as a freelancer. If you've never interviewed anyone, practice first. Call a friend who has specific expertise or knowledge and practice. See how it goes. Pay attention to the flow of the interview. Learn how to redirect the conversation when necessary and probe when additional questions or new paths come up in the conversation.

Interviewing skills are an essential part of being a successful freelancer. The nerves you feel during your first few will diminish as you get more practice. Most people will be flattered that you want to interview them. Business people see it as a public relations opportunity. With celebrities, well, it's part of their job. As for people who just might have an interesting story, most are happy to share.

Types of Interview: What Works Best?
The type of interview (in-person, phone, email) you choose will depend on a number of factors. Let's look at each.

In-Person

There's nothing better than an in-person interview and it is an absolute necessity for a profile piece. Location is important. While a Starbucks might be convenient, try to meet them on their turf. If you are interviewing an executive, go to their office. A celebrity? Try to go to their home or an entertainment venue. A chef? Go to the restaurant. The point is to go where they "live." Look around. What is on the walls? What does the environment say about the person and their interests? Is the kitchen spotless? A little messy? Though you might not want to say that there were dishes in the sink, these observations will make the person seem more "human" to you and hopefully allow the reader to truly get a feel for the person.

If you are doing a profile, consider trying to vary the interview venue to get a more comprehensive view. Try shadowing the interviewee for a day.

Dress appropriately. Forget the jeans unless you are absolutely sure that they are appropriate. An outdoor interview might qualify but ripped jeans just don't work. You want to appear professional. Business casual will usually suffice.

Recording the interview can make note-taking easier and more accurate as well as allowing you to participate more fully in the conversation. But remember you must have the interviewee's permission.

For an article in which you just want to get a couple of quotes and some information, though, an in-person interview may take up too much of their time and yours. Plus, additional costs are involved and, even if your travel expenses are reimbursed, the additional time has to be weighed against the fee.

Telephone interviews
Telephone interviews, to me, are the toughest. However you can let the conversation take its course, within the pre-determined time allotment. And you don't have travel costs. Make sure to do an equipment check first and if you are using a cell phone, check your service and make sure you have a full charge. There are apps for recording phone conversations and it's a good idea to use one. Just like in-person interviews, you'll need permission but you'll be happy to have the record when you write the article.

Email
The good news with email is that the interviewee can take their time and provide thoughtful answers. That's also the bad news because he or she can take their time. So if you use an email interview, make sure you make your deadline clear.

Email interviews also don't allow for any type of spontaneous comments or conversation. This may be okay depending on the type of article. Another downside is that you often get short, incomplete and not useful answers. You can then either choose to try again with follow-up questions or, forget it. That's why, unless it's a profile piece, you need multiple interviews.

Lining up the Interview
Often lining up the interview is a chicken and egg situation. If you're new to freelancing and want a strong pitch, it helps to have credible interviews set up. Unfortunately, that's not always possible without a firm assignment. If you're really lucky, the editor might suggest a few people who may be amenable to an interview. You just have to play it by ear.

I recommend trying an email first. Something short and polite.
For instance:

Dear Mr./Ms. Jones;
I am a freelance writer working on an article for (magazine title). The article is on innovations in the medical diagnostic field with a specific focus on _____. (If someone suggested you contact Mr./Ms. Jones, say so here.)
I understand that you have a great deal of expertise in this area and I would appreciate the opportunity to interview you for this article. My deadline is (xxx weeks away) and so if you have some time in the next few weeks, I would like to schedule some time, either in person or on the phone, to get your input.

Thank you for your time and consideration.

Sincerely,

Name
Phone
Email

People are busy. Give them a week to 10 days, if you can, to respond and then follow-up.

PR people can be a great resource to help set up an interview. They can also provide background material. The PR person may want to attend the interview, either in-person or on the phone and will mostly just stay in the background. Again, it's their job and if you make it easy for them, they will likely be willing and able to help you the next time.

Be Prepared!
There is nothing that will sabotage an interview faster than lack of preparation. Read everything you can on the person (within reason), the product or the service, before you develop your questions. You don't have to be the expert. After all that's why you're doing the interview. But you have to be educated.

Make sure your questions are prioritized from most important to least important in case you run out of time.

Do I have to verify quotes?

There's no clear-cut answer to this and it can be a slippery slope. Many journalists do not give their interviewee a chance to revise their quotes, relying instead on their ability to record and relate responses accurately. This is particularly true of investigative journalists.

If you ask editors, they will, almost always, say you do not have a responsibility to confirm quotes. That said, how many times have you run into people who hold a grudge against writers saying that they have been misquoted? None? You will.

So, what's a conscientious writer to do? Use common sense. I have had many interviewees ask to review the article. I say no, always (unless of course it is the client!). I do this for two reasons. First, reviewing my work is not their job. Secondly, once a writer turns in an article to an editor, all bets are off. The editor can cut and edit as they see fit although you may occasionally have the opportunity to review it prior to publication, you have no control over the finished product. So even if the interviewee does see, and approve, the article once you have completed your draft, there is no guarantee that this is what will finally find its way into print. Guess who is going to be blamed if they don't like the published article?

My goal is to provide information and I want to make sure it's as accurate as it can be. If the interviewee asks to see the quote(s), I will often do that. I have never had someone substantially change a quote although people have grumbled that I cut too much out. If they do want to substantially change the quote – and it doesn't work for the article – I just omit it.

Types of Questions
Questions, like answers, can take many forms and every interview should use a combination of these questions. Closed questions elicit short, focused answers, often just a yes or no. They can be effective in starting a conversation or to gain information to form additional questions. For instance, what college did you attend? Or, how many children do you have?

Open-ended questions on the other hand, allow for longer and more free-flowing answers, therefore encouraging more creativity and information. For instance, "When did you first know that your company would be a success?"

Mirror questions or statements are intended to encourage another person to expand on what they have said. For instance, "If I understand you correctly...." Use these statements to ensure that you have understood a response and to encourage the interviewee to correct your understanding or expand on their response.

Probing questions are used when you want or need more information on a particular topic. For instance, "Could you tell me more about..." or "Can you give me an example?" These are important. Learn to do them well.

The Interview
You have done your homework. You have your research and you have developed a good list of questions. Now what? There is a structure to most interviews that loosely follows the format below.

- Introduce yourself and the client/publication for which you are writing the article. Be prepared to answer questions such as circulation and audience.
- Try a little small talk to set the stage for a comfortable conversation. Even on the phone, a comment about the weather can help to set a friendly tone. Keep it short out of respect for their time and yours.
- Let the subject talk but stay in control. Since you're interviewing this individual, they presumably have extensive knowledge on their subject. That's good, but don't let them go too far afield. You'll run out of time and end up without the information you need.
- Ask the interviewee if there is anything else they'd like to add. Most say no but once in a while you come across an important point that can enhance the article.
- Ask if you can get back to them with any other questions and their preferred method of contact. Leave your contact information as well.

Interviews can be one of the most interesting parts of writing an article. Meeting new people, with different interests can expand your knowledge and lead to new ideas as you pursue your freelancing career. Enjoy them!

A few tips:

- Interview more than one person, preferably three or four, depending on the topic. This adds to credibility and fills in the blanks in case one interviewee cannot participate or the answers don't work.
- Listen to that nagging voice and do your own research to make sure what you are writing is correct. Despite your research and careful selection of interviewees, even the most knowledgeable people can be wrong. (If you find a problem, and you feel comfortable going back to the source, go ahead. If not, just don't use it.)
- Watch your time carefully. It can be tricky to balance your need to ask open-ended questions and to gather information, and time constraints – especially those dictated by the interviewee.
- Be clear and upfront with interviewee. What if the interviewee says that a comment is "off the record?" The person being interviewed knows you are writing an article so the assumption is that everything that is said is "on the record." If your interviewee asks if they can make a comment off the record, you can say yes – or no. But they can't, retroactively, say that something was off the record

after the interview. It's your call unless he/she specifically asks ahead of time.

- Establish goals for the interview to ensure that your article stays focused.
- Bring a camera if photos are not already available. Take pictures of all interviewees. You and the editor can decide which to use later.
- Leave the door wide open for additional communications for your current, or for future, articles.

Chapter 6
Writing: Watching the Words Flow

One of the first things you need to ask yourself is "can I write?" I'm going to assume that if you are this far, you can and have had some experience. But if you're unsure, or haven't done a lot of writing, it may be worthwhile to take a writing and/or editing course at a local college or university to add some polish.

Have an idea that you think will sell? Unless you're backlogged with paying assignments, start writing while the idea is fresh. You don't have to complete the article or even edit at this point. But it will help you draft a query or get a start when you're ready to write the piece.

It may sound like you're back in high school but an outline will help you stay on track as you begin to write. It doesn't have to be very detailed but, at a minimum, it should include an introductory sentence or paragraph (you can change it later), subheads, and bullets so you remember to include the pertinent points. An outline will also help you stay organized and help to ensure a smoother flow.

Almost without exception, publications will give you an assigned word count. Take these counts seriously. If the assignment is for 600 words that does not mean 400 or 800 words, no matter how wonderful you think those words may be. You have to be willing to cut as many of those wonderful words as necessary to meet the assignment specs. If you don't, the editor will and the last thing you want to do is to make their job harder. Writing to this count is a learned skill that will get easier the more you do.

If you find that you absolutely cannot do justice to the subject in the space allotted, try one more time to write tight. If it still doesn't work, call the editor. Maybe they'll let you do a two-part piece. Maybe they have some flexibility, especially online. If not, get your red pen out. At least you will have explored your options.

Quotes

Quotes are great. They help to add credibility to your research, to support your points or to feature the individual you are quoting. But be careful. They need to be exact. Period. Record them if possible and make sure to tell the subject that they are being recorded – it's not the law in every state, so know the law of your state. Federal law requires one-party consent and the journalist/ writer counts as the one-party. If you want to play it safe, be upfront with the other party.

Some people talk in sound bites. Others not so much. Use discretion in which quotes you incorporate. People generally talk more casually than they would if they were conscious of the fact that every word could appear in print. This is especially true if you are a good interviewer with a relaxed interviewee. So, if something doesn't sound right, either skip it or try to verify the quote. Your job is not to make people sound stupid or silly.

Style
A personal style (or "voice") is a tough thing to define. Some people use a more informal style (this book is a case in point). Others write more formally. A successful freelancer needs to be able to adapt to the style of the publication, media or client for whom they are writing. For instance, if you are writing advertising copy, the tone is usually lighter with a promotional bent and typically includes lots of glowing adjectives. A scientific article will have a more academic tone. A business article will fall in between.

If you are writing for a publication, it is your job to try to match their style as closely as possible. It can be a little confusing because styles can also vary within the same publication. Many, for instance, have a "back page" article where the challenge to the writer is to distill a subject to its essence, with clarity, sometimes humor, and often the writer's point of view, all in one page (usually about 750 words). This is a very different assignment than a feature that, in print, runs between 1,000 and 2,000 words in most trade publications. Read the publication carefully to understand their style.

Your style will depend on your client as well. A marketing agency for instance will have a more informal approach than a law firm. Read other material that your client has published to understand their style.

No Matter What Style

Correct grammar and spelling are important – always. Most magazines follow specific rules of style and grammar. Some follow the Associated Press (AP) style, some follow the Chicago Manual of Style and others, usually more academic journals, follow the American Psychological Association (APA) rules. Make sure you know what your assignment requires – even before you start writing. It will save you a lot of time later when you don't have to change abbreviations or other formatting styles. Even better, it will save the editor from either having to make the change (which does not bode well for future assignments) or send it back to you for a more complete edit.

Incorporating Interviews Into Your Article

If you have asked a good mix of types of questions in an interview, in a logical sequence, incorporating the answers into your article should be fairly straightforward. Do not, however, give in to the temptation to use answers to avoid writing. Unless you are doing a Q&A, the answers are there to support and add to your piece, not to replace it.

Look at the article visually (the editor will). Is it overloaded with long, dense quotes from either an interview or research? That can turn off a reader before they even get to your introductory sentence. Pace your article by interspersing long and short quotes.

Feature Articles
Feature articles are likely to be the focus of much of your freelancing career. You've heard the advice, "Tell them what you're going to say. Say it. Tell them what you said." It's basically the same thing in an article.

The "lead" or introduction should set the stage. This can, for instance, take the form of a personal story (Bill was 27 years old when...) or something that grabs the reader's attention (Seventy-eight percent of people are not aware that they.....Are you one of them?). The point is to start the article in a bold/intriguing/interesting way to entice the reader to keep reading.

For most articles (say 1,500 words or less), the article will move progressively from the introduction to a second paragraph that will include a kind of thesis, or statement. For instance, "Medical care is increasingly being offered in retail settings, including pharmacies and clinics that offer walk-in services and geographic convenience."

The article will then move into more complex content where your research and interviews are used to support your thesis. In the above example, I would include statistics on the growth of retail medical care (there is an association for that!) and a quote (or multiple quotes) from executives from an urgent care center or retail drug store that has a health care center. This section will typically be the longest, with multiple paragraphs that tell the story.

A strong conclusion is important. Don't leave the reader hanging.

If possible, put the article down for a couple of days to get some distance and a better perspective. Have a friend read it. The point is to make sure it flows and you haven't left out important information or left important questions unanswered.

Writing a How-To Article
The structure of a how-to is similar to a feature but the components are different. First choose a compelling topic. A narrow focus is fine as long as you have an outlet in mind – a firm assignment is even better.

How-to articles are done chronologically. Your introduction will explain what you are going to make/build/create or accomplish with the article.

That is, step 1, 2, etc. Depending on the publication and the detail required to be clear, the topic may require very simple steps that can most appropriately be explained with bullet points. More complicated projects will naturally require more content.

Be concise. You don't want the reader to get bogged down in superfluous details when they're trying to get something done. When you're reviewing your article, try to anticipate the questions that might arise. Finally, follow the instructions – to the letter – yourself. Better yet, have a friend follow your instructions and watch carefully. That's how you will know if it works.

Profiles
The foundation for a profile usually lies in the interview. Before you meet with the individual, do your homework! Then, and only then, develop your questions.

In a profile piece, the purpose of the introductory paragraph is to explain, clearly, why the reader should care about this person. Are they a movie star? An executive of a rapidly growing company? An inventor of a technological breakthrough? Or are they just someone with whom the reader can identify?

Next, set the stage with some background information. If the person is a key executive in an industry, what was their education? How did they get their start in the industry? Was it a childhood dream? What jobs did they hold on the way to their current position?

Now go back to why he or she is important. Provide details on their current position and why they have an impact. Include important quotes. And as much as the person might have expounded on a topic in the interview, don't let them ramble on in print. You might for instance ask what the most important part of their job is or their philosophy about hiring.

Finally, look ahead. What are the executive's plans? For themselves or the company? Is the technology expected to disrupt the industry? How and when? Depending on the answers, these answers often turn out to be a great conclusion to the profile!

Profiles always include photographs of the person, the technology, whatever. Big publications send a photographer. Most of the time when writing for trade publications, you will be able to get these pictures from the company if you can't take quality shots yourself. Smaller publications of any sort will probably ask if you have your own camera.

Q&As (Question & Answers)
Q&As can be both easier and tougher to write than other types of articles. On the one hand, much of your word count will be verbatim quotes. On the other hand, it is your responsibility as the author to make sure there is a recognizable theme and that the answers, whether from one person or multiple people, flow and are interesting.

Interviews, especially good ones, tend to yield much more than you can use. Understand that you will probably have to cut – a lot. Ellipses – three dots – can be useful to indicate that the quote was truncated.

When doing a Q&A, you should start with a set of questions centered on the assigned topic. But don't be rigid. People often take unexpected paths in conversation that can add interesting content, but be ready though to bring the interviewee back on track when necessary. Consider asking questions that will allow the reader to relate to the interviewee. For instance, in a business magazine, you may ask something about trends and how they impact the industry in general. If you are interviewing an actor, readers will likely want to know how they got their start. Q&As are fun, but not as easy as they seem.

Newspaper Articles

A news story is written in an "inverted pyramid." Imagine an editor cutting the story for space. The editor will cut from the bottom up. When completed, it should look like this:

- The first paragraph is the lead. Use the first line to hook the reader. Then include who, what, where, why and when.
- Second/third paragraphs should include the essential facts
- Move into quotes and other supporting material
- Other general and/or background information

- A strong last concluding sentence.

Writer's Block
This is from The Writing Life, in the April 29, 2013 issue The *New Yorker* by author John McPhee. The article is titled "Draft No. 4 Replacing the words in boxes." (It's worth reading the whole article).

> *"Dear Joel: You are writing, say, about a grizzly bear. No words are forthcoming. For six, seven, ten hours no words have been forthcoming. You are blocked, frustrated, in despair. You are nowhere, and that's where you've been getting. What do you do? You write, 'Dear Mother.' And then you tell your mother about the block, the frustration, the ineptitude, the despair. You insist that you are not cut out to do this kind of work. You whine. You whimper. You outline your problem, and you mention that the bear has a fifty-five-inch waist and a neck more than thirty inches around but could run nose-to-nose with Secretariat. You say the bear prefers to lie down and rest. The bear rests fourteen hours a day. And you go on like that as long as you can. And then you go back and delete the 'Dear Mother' and all the whimpering and whining, and just keep the bear."*

The point is to just start writing. Staring at a blank page is intimidating and de-motivating. If you can't start at the beginning, start in the middle. The important thing is to just do it! (with all due credit to Nike)

The words don't always flow. In fact, sometimes it's more like moving through mud. Everyone has those days. Take a walk. Call a friend (hopefully a fellow author). Just walk away from your desk. But not for too long.

A few more thoughts on writing non-fiction:
- Shorter is better. Shorter words and shorter sentences are easier to read. Write tight. I can't say this enough.
- Use appropriate detail. It's not just a dog – the dog has a name.
- Be judicious in your use of quotes. You don't have to use them all.
- Subheads are your friend.
- Consolidate your sources when you can so you don't have to reintroduce them later in the article.
- Read other articles on the subject. They can be inspiring.
- Be careful. Details can serve both to make the article more interesting as well as to bog it down. Be careful.
- No matter what you are writing, if at all possible, put it down for a couple of days, then reread it. Resist the temptation to just say "Whew, that's done," and not do a careful review.

Before you hit the send button, be sure:

- You've edited *very* carefully.

- You have all your pictures and graphics.
- You have supplied captions with all pictures and graphics.
- You have your sources organized should any questions arise.
- You have a short (50-60 words), and a shorter (2 sentences) bio to include.

Writing is hard. It's sometimes hard to get motivated. Hard to find the time if you have a "day job." Hard to resist distractions. Hard to stay motivated when trying to get new assignments. But it's not a bad life.

Chapter 7
Editing: A Necessary Skill

There are two good reasons to get really good at editing.

First, editors appreciate a well-edited document. A freelancer who turns in a good article that is well-polished is likely to receive new assignments. It's that simple. That doesn't mean that an error will cost your future assignments. But the better your article is from an editing point of view, the happier the editor is going to be. That's important to your career.

Second, there are freelance editing jobs that can pay pretty well. If you're good, the repeat business potential can be very good. These jobs can come from for profit and not-profit companies, publishers, advertising agencies or other businesses that rely on content. Check with your local writer's association (try Facebook and LinkedIn groups) for potential customers. Or, again, try Google. A recent search on "copy editing jobs freelance" resulted in many opportunities.

Here are just the first few:

Freelance Copy Editing Jobs Online - Upwork
https://www.upwork.com/o/jobs/browse/skill/copy-editing/

Freelance Copy Editor Jobs | Glassdoor
https://www.glassdoor.com/Job/freelance-copy-editor-jobs-SRCH_KO0,21.htm

Online Copy Editor Jobs - Monster.com
https://www.monster.com/jobs/q-online-copy-editor-jobs.aspx

Freelance Editor Jobs, Employment | Indeed.com
http://www.indeed.com/q-Freelance-Editor-jobs.html

A caveat: I have not personally reviewed or worked with any of these but these are just a few of many listings.

Types of Editing

There are three basic types of editing - copy editing, line editing, and developmental editing.

- *Copy Editing*
  Copy editing refers to grammar, spelling, and punctuation. These rules are not a matter of opinion. Creative spelling is not an option despite what your second-grader may tell you. As far as the rules, find out what style the publication uses – such as APA, Chicago Manual of Style and AP (see resources) and follow the rules. It's an objective process, with little room for judgment. You can also find a guide of handwritten copy editing marks from NY Book Editors –

www.nybookeditors.com/2013/06/copyediting-marks

- *Line Editing*
  This is most typically used in prose and looks at voice, readability, style, sentence flow, and other components that contribute to good writing.

- *Developmental Editing*
  In non-fiction, this refers to the process by which the article is reviewed for structure and content. Inconsistencies, logic errors and more content-based issues should be addressed.

Freelance editors will usually specialize in one of these areas.

Editing Tips

- Read the paper aloud as if you're reading a story. Listen for errors. Listen for incomplete phrases, sentences, and ideas. Better yet, have someone read it to you.
- Give yourself some time, preferably a day or more between when you've finished writing and when you edit. You're more likely to catch errors.
- All writers have patterns of errors. Know what yours are and watch for them.

- Know what style you are expected to use and have the guide nearby. Check everything about which you have even the slightest question.
- Consider creating your own style sheet (that follows acceptable rules) but which will allow you to quickly reference common questions – or bad habits you may have.
- Be careful with slang and catchphrases. When in doubt, don't use them. They are rarely appropriate.
- Consider having someone who is unfamiliar with the topic read the piece. Some terms specific to the audience will be okay but you want the article to be readable and clear to someone not familiar with the subject.

Some Common Mistakes

Grammar and spelling checks are a great first step, but that's all they are. They may get the obvious but more subtle errors need the human touch.

- Look for consistency of tenses.
- Define all abbreviations the first time they are mentioned, even if you think the audience will know the abbreviation. Let the editor decide.
- Spell out single digits. Subsequent numbers (10 and up) should be written as numerals except abbreviations of measurement and large numbers (e.g. 6 million). Be consistent.

- Watch to, too and two; their, there and they're; your and you're; its and it's. If you don't know the difference, look it up.
- Sentence fragments are my downfall. But sometimes they're okay.

Editing is hard. But it's necessary and it's important to a successful freelancing career.

Working with Your Editor

For editors, assigning an article to a freelancer is only a first step. Their job is to provide accurate, engaging articles of interest to their readers. For them, the process kicks into full gear only after the article is submitted.

Most editors are pretty easy to work with. (Depending on the publication you many even be able to end a sentence with a preposition!) The editor's job is to make sure the article has no errors, the length is correct; the article fits their mission, and has the proper formatting and style. Then they have to approve the layout, decide on graphics and make sure it's all done on time. Their livelihood depends on doing it well. It's a big job, especially when they have many articles to review and are on deadline. So, the more you can do to make your article mistake-free, the more valuable you are as a writer.

If you have written an article on behalf of a client, you have probably already gone through a series of edits.

Once the client has approved the piece, it needs to go to the editor who, again, can make any changes the editor wants. The problem is that anything other than minor editorial changes may cause an issue with your client. It is your responsibility to control your client's expectations and make sure they understand that the editor has the last word. If they don't agree, you may have to pull the article.

To develop a lasting relationship with an editor:

- Make sure your articles are submitted early or on time;
- Follow the agreed - upon specifications including length;
- Know the style of the publication and follow it;
- Make sure if you have photos or graphics, they are attached and include captions. Make sure that you have included the proper attributions; and
- Include an updated bio of the author (two-three sentences as well as a longer one (about 65 words) giving the editor a choice.

Editors may ask you to revise an article. That can mean anything from a total rewrite to making relatively minor changes in the text. Most of the time, there is no advantage to arguing. Just make sure you understand what they want to change and why. You don't want to rewrite again or make the process more difficult.

There's no question that it can be tough to have another person make changes on a piece on which you have worked so hard. Get over it. The option is for you to take back the article. Then you might have to deal with contractual issues and you will definitely have to deal with bad feelings. It's hard to imagine a situation where this is worthwhile for a freelancer looking to grow a business.

Sidebar
You don't think typos matter so much? Consider these samples from mentalfloss.com.

1. NASA'S MISSING HYPHEN
The damage: $80 million
Hyphens don't usually score high on the list of most important punctuation. But a single dash led to absolute failure for NASA in 1962 in the case of Mariner 1, America's first interplanetary probe. The mission was simple: get up close and personal with close neighbor Venus. But a single missing hyphen in the coding used to set trajectory and speed caused the craft to explode just minutes after takeoff. *2001: A Space Odyssey* novelist Arthur C. Clarke called it "the most expensive hyphen in history."

2. THE CASE OF THE ANTIQUE ALE
The damage: $502,996
A missing 'P' cost one sloppy (and we'd have to surmise ill-informed) eBay seller more than half-a-mill on the 150-year-old beer he was auctioning. Few collectors

knew a bottle of Allsopp's Arctic Ale was up for bid, because it was listed as a bottle of *Allsop's* Arctic Ale. One eagle-eyed bidder hit a payday of *Antiques Roadshow* proportions when he came across the rare booze, purchased it for $304, then immediately re-sold it for $503,300.

3. THE BIBLE PROMOTES PROMISCUITY
The damage: $4590 (and eternal damnation)

Not even the heavenly father is immune to occasional inattention to detail. In 1631, London's Baker Book House rewrote the 10 Commandments when a missing word in the seventh directive declared, "Thou shalt commit adultery." Parliament was not singing hallelujah; they declared that all erroneous copies of the Good Book—which came to be known as "The Wicked Bible"—be destroyed and fined the London publisher 3000 pounds.

Chapter 8
Marketing Yourself

Okay, you're a freelance writer. You know it. Your family and friends know it. Now what? Well, the phone is unlikely to ring and your email box is unlikely to fill with assignments unless other people know what you can do. That's your job too.

It's not easy. "Selling yourself" is uncomfortable for most people. If you're making calls, make sure you have a script and practice so that it sounds conversational and natural. And then make sure you have follow-up material you can send.

A well-written email, to the right person can help generate business. Queries (see chapter 3) can generate assignments and, for those who are new to freelancing or even new to a specific niche, there is always the option of writing on spec to begin to build a portfolio. Other ways to create a portfolio include:

- Volunteer to write for a non-profit – especially one with which you are familiar.
- Do you know a small-business owner? Volunteer to write their next brochure or new pages on their website. Charging a small amount is possible too.
- Get to know some local graphic designers with whom you might be able to work on joint projects.

- Still working a day job? Can you write something for your employer?
- Take a writing course. You'll meet people, get better at your trade, and create a few writing samples.
- Local publications always need help, though the pay is minimal if any. Be ready to pitch ideas in case they don't have an assignment ready.

Finding a Niche

Good freelancers can write about almost anything – except perhaps medical, scientific or technical pieces that require specific knowledge. Being a generalist is not a bad thing. I've written on everything from finding a mortgage and construction loans to insurance, database marketing and horse shows. While I didn't necessarily have a lot of experience in these areas, I knew how to find out what I needed.

Having said that, my concentration was really marketing. Over time I was able to build up not only a client base but good relationships with editors who would call me if they needed an expert for a staff-written article or a bylined piece (an article that has author attribution). Or a quote, which my clients appreciate as well.

Do you have experience in a specific industry? For instance, a children's librarian has a great background to begin to place articles in publications for librarians, children, or schools – even children's book reviews for local, regional or national publications. If you spent years in the industrial sector, there are publications looking for relevant case studies. Did you homeschool your children? Publications about homeschooling are always looking for new ideas. Do you have a hobby to which you have devoted time and energy? There are magazines for that. You get the gist. A niche can form the foundation for your business and can often provide a reasonably steady income.

Website

You need a website. Even if people meet you in person, the likelihood is that they will ask for a site that they can peruse at their leisure. It does not have to be fancy. A few graphics to make it look good will do and there are many resources that can provide templates and make the process fairly simple. What you do need is excellent content. After all, that's what you're selling.

On a writer's website, content will include, at a minimum:

- Contact information;
- List of publications where your work has appeared;
- Writing samples;
- Links to published works (if you have approval from the publication);
- Updates on the home page regarding recently published articles or projects; and
- Links to your professional social media such as LinkedIn, Twitter and Facebook.

Social media is another great tool to market yourself – while keeping your expenses at a minimum. Consider starting or at least participating in a blog(s) in your area(s) of interest. Research and participate in relevant groups on LinkedIn and Facebook.

Looking for Work
Often, when people leave their companies on good terms, they can turn right around and offer their services to their former employer. The employer wins since they have a writer who is familiar with their business and you win because you can hit the ground running.

Advertising, marketing and public relations agencies (which actually have always been my biggest clients) often use freelancers as either backup for business peaks or to fill in areas where they may not have specific expertise. For instance, I've done work for agencies that were expert at marketing strategies and advertising but public relations was out of their wheelhouse. Having someone who understood their industry – and PR - was a real benefit to them.

Depending on the size of the agency, your contact will vary. In a small agency, it may be the president or owner. In a bigger agency, there may be a content manager or creative director. If you're interested in PR, there maybe be someone in charge of that department. In any case, make sure you have an introductory letter to agencies. It might go something like this:

Dear (name):

As a fellow communications professional, I understand how important it is to meet deadlines. When you're busy with client work, that can be tough. I would like to offer my services as a backup for those times when your company is inundated with any project, large or small.

For more than 25 years I have partnered with agencies to support their efforts on behalf of their clients. My portfolio includes traditional public relations services – including bylined articles and press releases. I have worked with clients on marketing communications essentials that include website copy development, newsletters, brochures, sales sheets, case studies, scripts, research, special reports, white papers, and more.
(note: if you have done these things for an employer, that counts too. Include those things you can support.)
In addition, I have worked with agencies to promote their own capabilities, by developing a strong media presence through bylined articles in vertical industry trade publications. The goal is to work together to establish your agency as a resource for staff-written pieces, bylined pieces and speaker placements at industry and general business events.

Whether you would like to expand your scope or you need outsourced support on an hourly or project basis –I can back you up.

To learn more, please contact me at (email and phone contact info). I'd be happy to discuss your specific needs and how we might work together.

Sincerely,
Name

Contacting Companies
As is the case with agencies, when contacting businesses, the tricky part is to make sure you have the right individual. In big companies, this is usually the person who heads up their marketing and/or public relations departments. In smaller companies, it may be the president.

Create a targeted email that shows you have researched the company and understand what it does. If I were targeting employee benefits firms, for instance, I would probably address the letter to the marketing manager or president, depending on the size. It might go something like this:

Dear (name):
Employee benefits are getting more complicated. Yet, the very companies who need the most help are often the ones least likely to be able to afford a full-time benefits manager.

That's where you come in. First, however, these companies need to know about your services and your expertise.

Public relations can help. When the media is aware of your company, your products, your people, your expertise and your accomplishments, they will share your expertise with their readers.

XYZ Company has been partnering with clients for more than X years, helping them to get the word out through press releases, articles in trade publications and establishing media relationships that can lead to interviews and additional exposure to potential clients.

I would be pleased to further discuss, at your convenience, how we may work together.

Thank you.
Name
Phone
Email

If there is a local Chamber of Commerce in your area, try going to one of their meetings. It may not be the group you want (they're often comprised of smaller, local businesses) but you can usually attend at least one meeting without joining. Chambers in larger urban areas may have larger corporate members. You may even be able to get a speaking engagement, perhaps on how to develop and implement a public relations strategy. Don't worry, you're not giving anything away. The fact is that most businesses are either too busy or lack the expertise to do it themselves.

If you are trying to focus in a specific industry, say manufacturing, your area may have a local chapter of a national organization. See what meetings are being held in that area. Check out local writer's conferences as well.

Cross-sell and Upsell to Current Customers
If you have spent any time in marketing, you have probably heard that it is more expensive to acquire a new customer than to sell a current customer. It's true. Cross-selling (selling additional items to a current customer) and upselling are terms that mean, simply, that you go to an existing customer (who presumably is happy with your work) and offer additional services. Your learning curve is lessened or eliminated entirely and your productivity will be higher than with a new client.

Let's say you have a client for whom you have developed a series of promotional brochures. How about proposing a white paper or additional website content? Even if they say no, they will appreciate your initiative and may call you next time something comes up. It's a lot easier than cold calling.

Pricing your Services
When writing directly for a publication, price is usually pre-determined. Better-known writers may make more

money but the publication sets the rate. That's not necessarily the case when working directly for organizations that will typically ask you for a proposal. *Writer's Market* offers a valuable "How Much Should I Charge" pay rate chart, used by freelancers to see how much similar projects will cost. The chart is broken down into Advertising & Public Relations; Book Publishing; Business; Computer, Internet & Technical; Editorial/Design Packages; Educational & Literary Services; Film, Video, TV, Radio & Stage; Magazines & Trade Journals; Medical/Science; Newspapers; Nonprofit; and Politics/Government. Each category is then broken down into per hour, and other pricing schemes and, within that, high, low and average rates.

Pricing – Factors to Consider

- Will there be multiple meetings? In person or on the phone? Will travel be involved?
- Is there a quick turnaround required?
- How technical is the subject?
- Will the client need to mark-up your services?
- How big is the client?
- What is the nature of the project?

There are some good reasons to take less than you would like. A large project may reduce your hourly rate. If you do work for an agency that bills the client directly, they need to make money as well so freelancers (including myself) will often discount their rates. The other side of the coin is that if you're busy and have to outsource your own work, it is reasonable to expect that your subcontractors offer you a discount though not all will. Or perhaps you will have a steep learning curve to get up to speed. It might be worthwhile for you to take that on without additional charges if there is additional potential business. Your client is unlikely to be willing to take on this expense.

Subcontractors and out-sourcing are double-edged swords. On one hand you can handle more work – even at a smaller profit. But unless you've worked with the person successfully in the past, the management time it will take to ensure that their work is up to your standards can be significant. You will need to carefully edit all work that goes out under your name. Having more work than you can handle is not the worst problem in the freelance writing world, but it does require management.

No matter how you charge for your services – hourly, project, retainer – your rate should reflect the competitive marketplace, your experience and background, your client's budget, and your targeted hourly rate.

Advertising

Maybe. It might work but it's expensive. Emails and phone calls are a lot less expensive and feedback is more immediate. In any case, don't start off with a big, splashy ad. Rather start with a small ad in a targeted publication. For instance, if you feel comfortable in the business market, how about an ad in a local business publication?

Try setting daily and weekly goals. Ten new emails a week. Two queries a week. One meeting a month. Eventually you will build up a pipeline and have a steady stream of income. If you get busy, the temptation is to cut back your marketing efforts. That's usually a mistake. You want to be ready for the inevitable business valleys.

How long will it take to see the checks in your mailbox? In the end, it depends on you.

Finding Lists of Businesses

If you want to work in the business community, there are many sources of potential contacts. Business magazines and newspapers often publish lists of top 100 companies. Or top 25 in specific industries. Check the library if you don't get these publications in print, electronically or both. Google specific industries with geographic parameters that make sense.

Chapter 9
The Business of Freelancing

You need to take your business seriously. The business end may not be fun but it is a necessary part of being a freelancer. Have a designated place to work – whether it is in your home, a coffee shop or an office. Present yourself professionally when dealing with a client. Keep accurate and up-to-date records. Stick to deadlines.

Starting a freelance business is not free. You need a computer and to keep it up and running. Clients can take an extra month or two to pay so be prepared financially for a lull in cash flow. Business can vary from month to month. You need insurance. You need to file tax returns, whether you pay for the software or an accountant. You need to eat. Bottom line? Be prepared. A bank account with three months of expenses set aside is probably a minimum – especially for those just starting out.

On Assignment
It's exciting to get an assignment. But this is not the time to celebrate. If the publication does not offer to send an email confirming the specifications, take it upon yourself to do so. It can save a lot of time and aggravation going forward plus it helps you to establish yourself as a professional in the eyes of the editor.

The email will go something like this:

Dear Jane/John:
Thank you for the assignment to write (article title/working title) for (publication name).
Per the specifications we discussed, I will submit a (# of words) article to include (Interviews? Photos?) by (deadline).
Add any other specifics you many have discussed, including payment amount and terms, and what rights are being purchased
Thank you again.

Short and sweet but professional and necessary.

Some publications and some companies require a contract. Most are pretty standard. Read them anyway. Look for terms regarding acceptance, rights (see side bar page 102) and payment terms and make sure you understand them. Most of the time negotiations are possible. Many companies will also require a non-disclosure agreement (NDA) that basically says that any information you receive from them is not to be shared. This protects them against you sharing information with a competitor. I just sign them.

Next step – do what you said you were going to do, when you said you were going to do it. If issues arise, and they will on occasion, try to find an alternative before you contact the editor if possible. For instance, if you have difficulty getting a promised interview, try to find an alternative, such as another interviewee with similar credentials. Let the editor know of any change as soon as possible. If you find that you are unable to meet the deadline, let the editor know. Perhaps they can push the article to the next issue or can give you a little more time. But they need to know in advance for layout, ad/editorial ratios, etc. They'll appreciate the heads up.

Ok, you've written the article, it was accepted and payment is due. You haunt your mailbox. Just bills and promotions. What now? First, check your agreement. Did they say payment was on publication? If so, remember that many publications work 60-90 days ahead. On acceptance? In 30 days? If the publication has not sent payment under the agreed upon terms, assume first that it is just an error. Send a quick note to the editor, saying that your understanding was that payment would be received within xx days. Attach a copy of the invoice and ask if there is anyone else you should contact (e.g. accounting). If the editor says yes, do so, again with a copy of the invoice attached and reference the discussion with the editor.

Collecting payment isn't fun and it may take multiple efforts but remember that 1) it's your money and you worked for it and 2) the people you talk to, unless they own the company, aren't paying with their own money. They want to get your bill off their desk almost as much as you want to get paid.

Payment

Publications differ in terms of what they pay and what rights they purchase. *Ladies Home Journal* for instance is listed in *Writer's Market* as paying $2,000-$4,000 for 2,000 to 3,000 words. Sounds great. But if you're new, this is a real stretch. Other publications, including trades, sometimes pay as little as $.10 a word. Content mills pay as little as $.01/word. Some pay only in copies of the publication in which your article appears. Most pay somewhere between. (Note: usually the word count is based on the final version.)

Publications also differ on when they pay.

What Did They Buy?

- **First rights** – The publication has the right to be the first to publish your material in a particular medium (such as a print publication). Be careful here if you have "published" the piece on a website, even your own, the publication might consider that the article has been previously published.

- **One-time** or **first North American serial rights** – The publication has the right to publish your story once or the right to publish your story for the first time in North America. This is good news. After publication it's yours.

- **All rights** – You cannot resell an article if you've signed these away.

- **Electronic rights** - This is the right to publish your work on the Internet or electronically. This can often be negotiated especially if it is in addition to print rights.

- **Reprint** or **second serial rights** - This is the right to publish a previously published article a second time.

Some pay on acceptance (though this is typically after any author edits that are required), others on publication. Both are legitimate but consider that on publication can be a problem. First, you have no control over when the article is published. So, if there is not room in a particular issue, or the next or the next, you are going to have to wait. Also, if your agreement includes "first North American serial rights," a publication delay will also delay your ability to repurpose an article.

Repurposing
If the publisher has agreed to one-time or first North American serial rights or no rights at all, you have the opportunity to increase your income by repurposing your article. Let's say you wrote an article on employee benefits. You wrote it for an accounting firm that serves a broad range of verticals. The first article was for an insurance magazine but the content is applicable to other industries, like utilities, retail or almost any other business category.

A caveat: make sure that the publications are not competitive and reach different audiences. It is not worth annoying an editor or losing a client. When in doubt, I've asked. Most of the time it's fine. If not, I drop it. Be sure to tell any subsequent outlets where the article has been published.

If you do place an article in another non-competitive publication, you will need to do some rewriting, especially the lead, conclusion and any examples to tailor it for the new publication. But this isn't hard and can get you double or triple duty from the same article. And if you're doing this for a client, they'll be even happier.

Working With Corporate Clients
Writing for businesses is different, though often more profitable, than writing directly for a publication. The variety of work is probably the biggest difference (see Chapter 1 on Writing Opportunities) but so is the relationship between you and your client. When you are working for an editor, it is typically on a project (or article) basis. When you are done, it's done until the next time.

With business relationships you have additional opportunities to "create" work. Not busy work – real work. For instance, if you are writing and placing articles for your client, your skills at writing effective queries can make you a valuable asset. The more you get to know the company – their people, products and services, markets, and their business – the more ideas you should be able to develop as to how your writing skills can advance their business – within their budget. Article content can be repurposed into blog posts. And the more you can do that, the happier they will be. The lesson I've learned over the years is that, within reason, higher prices can be justified by your client's business success.

Pricing for a corporate relationship can take different forms. Project rates are obvious and are typically priced based on the hourly rate you have set for yourself and how many hours you think the project will take. A price range (again, within reason) is usually fine. You don't always know at the start of the project, how many interviews will be required, or how much research you will need beyond what the company supplies.

Hourly rates are another option. The problem here is that neither you nor your client will have a good grip on the ultimate cost. When I do hourly rates, I always provide a range of hours. You can always add a caveat that says you will get pre-approval if the number of hours exceeds x.

Many people love retainers. I do have a few retainer clients but it is always based on experience. That is, with a new client, I will often provide a three-month plan, with a monthly fee and projects to be completed. Then at the end of ninety days, we meet to review the pricing and work output to determine if my hourly estimate has worked – for my client as well as for myself.

Just as publications don't like their articles appearing in a competitive publication, businesses will almost always ask that you not work for a direct competitor, especially if you are working on a retainer. Whether or not you agree depends on what the relationship is worth to you.

Chapter 10
Remember - It's a Business

It may be fun and you may spend much of your working life in your slippers but it's still a business.

Let's assume you're not independently wealthy and that you can't afford to keep an accountant and a lawyer on retainer. Well, take heart. You really don't need extensive professional assistance but help at the initial stages of the business is a good idea.

There are plenty of software packages available that are designed for small businesses. They're not hard to use and can handle most of what you need such as accounts payable (the bills you owe to others), accounts receivable (the amount others owe you), invoicing, and the ability to track income and expenses. If you already do your own taxes, you may want to try your hand at your business return.

Having said that, it will probably benefit you to pay for a meeting with an accountant to make sure that your books are structured properly, to answer any questions you may have about getting started and to make sure you are off on the right foot.

Consulting a lawyer at the start of your business can help you get organized and make important initial decisions such as how to structure your business. Most freelancers opt for a sole proprietorship rather than the corporate route because of additional cost and complexity. There are advantages however to incorporating including limited liability. Your attorney will be able to help you sort this out. It's also a good idea to have an attorney who knows you and your business in case other matters arise. You may, for instance, want your attorney to review a contract.

Don't forget insurance. Health insurance is the most obvious – and most expensive. But you may need other insurance policies. Liability insurance covers you against legal action related to you work, such as a mistake that causes damage to your client. Check your homeowners or renter's insurance to see if business assets are covered in case of theft or damage. Talk to an insurance broker to understand what is available and relevant.

While it's tempting to use friends when possible, this is not always the right decision. You want to maintain a professional relationship. Try calling a writer's association or ask other writers for a recommendation.

Home Offices
The good news about home offices – whether in a bedroom or a study – is that you don't have to pay rent and, of course, you get to work in your pajamas. The bad news is that you're working in your bedroom and you don't get out much. Take stock of yourself. Are you a self-

starter? Can you ignore the pile of laundry? Do you have the self-restraint to say no to lunch invitations from well-meaning friends who, quite simply, don't take working at home as seriously as they take working in an office?

Social media (and computer games) can sap hours a day. Resist the temptation. If you're finding it difficult to focus, don't just sit there and stare at an empty page. Take a walk. Take a break. But limit it to 15-30 minutes – then get back to work!

If you choose to work from your home, most people prefer a dedicated space (which is also necessary for a tax deduction). Wherever you choose to work, make sure it is conducive to productivity. (Some people can work in their pajamas, for others jeans are just fine. There are people who choose/need to get dressed in even casual work attire to put themselves "in the mood.")

Some people can live quite well in a more cluttered space. Others prefer organization. The key is to make the space productive so when you sit down to work, you are not wasting time cleaning up or looking through piles on your desk.

If working at home is not an option, there are office spaces that are not very expensive. Shared office space and other similar real estate are really quite reasonable, but make sure to check on additional services such as use of a conference room. For most freelancers, any rent takes a big chunk out of your income. Coffee shops (as long as you don't take advantage of them – they are a commercial entity that makes its money on turnover and coffee sales), libraries and other public spaces can work well.

Other Start-up Necessities
You need business cards. They don't have to be expensive and there are plenty of places on line that do a good job. Make sure you use good card stock, a legible font (don't get too fancy) and include a company name (if any), your name and your contact number. If you specialize in specific niche(s) add that too, perhaps on the back of the card. Make sure the cards are always up to date.

You may not need paper stationery or a fancy logo but you do need professional looking letterhead that you can use for emails and invoicing. It can be as simple as a template on your computer.

You need a way of keeping your records, preferably with good, easy to use, software.

Measuring Success
Success means different things to different people. Some people start a freelancing business with the goal of a six-figure income though for most freelancers this is a lofty goal. That's great but understand that this kind of money from freelancing means working just as hard, if not harder, making the same money in a corporate

environment. Yes you have a little more freedom but you also have many "bosses" whom you must answer to and you need to take that seriously. They do.

Some people want a steady income with a livable wage. Others are looking for a way to generate a part-time income on their own time while focusing on family life. Your success depends on your goals, drive and your talent.

Many people say that working on your own means you can say no. That's true. If there is someone you don't want to work with, a project that doesn't fit your skill set – you can say no. But you're not going to want to.

I think that the real advantage of freelancing is the ability to say yes. To have enough control of your own time to take on those projects that are interesting to you, even if they're not the most profitable. To lend a hand to a non-profit whose mission is important to you and to do so at a minimal charge if any. To go to a daytime soccer game. To say yes to a friend who wants to have lunch, with the understanding that you may have to work late that night. To work with people you like and projects that challenge you. In the end, that's what makes it all worthwhile.

Resources

There are good resources for new and experienced freelancers, many of which are available for free or for minimal cost. The following list includes just a few. Your imagination and Google will produce thousands more.

Style guides (from Wikipedia)
The Chicago Manual of Style
http://www.chicagomanualofstyle.org/home

A Manual for Writers of Research Papers, Theses, and Dissertations (Kate L. Turabian)
www.press.uchicago.edu/books/turabian/manual/index.html

Publication Manual of the American Psychological Association http://www.apastyle.org/

MLA Handbook for Writers of Research Papers
www.mla.org/Publications/Bookstore/Nonseries/MLA-Handbook-Eighth-Edition

For journalism

- *The Associated Press Stylebook*. By the Associated Press (AP).

- *The New York Times Manual of Style and Usage*. By Allan M. Siegal and William G. Connolly.
- *The Wall Street Journal Guide to Business Style and Usage*, by Ronald J. Alsop and the Staff of the *Wall Street Journal*.

Freelancing

American Writers and Artists (www.awaionline.com)– If you sign up, expect lots of promotional emails but there is a great deal of good information.

Make a Living Writing (www.makealivingwriting.com) - "Practical Help for Hungry Writers" – sign up for free and get a free e-book, "100+ Freelance Writing Questions Answered."

The Great Courses (www.thegreatcourses.com) - in addition to courses on history, food, etc., a recent catalog offered a course titled Writing Creative Nonfiction.

All Indie Writers (www.allindiewriters.com) - resources in categories including writing forums, writer's markets, freelance writing blogs, job boards and freelance marketplaces, books for freelance writers, social media tools for freelance writers, writing and editing tools, and more.

Every Writers Resource
(http://www.everywritersresource.com/freelance-writing-resouces/)

Markets

Writer's Digest – There's a good reason this book has been an invaluable resource for so many years. Good information and a good list of markets including guidelines and excellent advice.

Freelance Success (www.freelancesuccess.com) - "The Ultimate Resource for Established, Professional Non-Fiction Writers" ($99/year subscription)

Scripted (www.scripted.com)

Writing Advertising Copy

Entrepreneur - The Ten Commandments of Great Copywriting, Rosser Reeves
(https://www.entrepreneur.com/article/164812)

NY Times - How to Write a Profile Feature Article
(www.nytimes.com/learning/students/writing/voices.html)

Writing Direct Mail Copy
Entrepreneur - 5 Tips for Producing Direct Mail Copy that Sells, Craig Simpson
(https://www.entrepreneur.com/article/230745)

Associations
Want to write about cats? There's a group for that. Dogs? Yep. Science Fiction? That too. There is a group for almost any category of writing that you can think of.

Many regions have a writer's group that offers educational and meeting opportunities. Two sites that offer good lists include:
Writer's Relief (http://writersrelief.com/writers-associations-organizations/)

The Balance (https://www.thebalance.com/list-of-writers-associations-1360811.)

If you don't see a group within a reasonable distance, or that doesn't address your particular interest, again, Google is your friend.

Education
Most colleges and universities have some type of writing course, whether on journalism, creative writing, non-fiction and chances are you are within a reasonable distance of one, if not more. Another place to look is the Association of Writers and Writing Programs (www.awpwriter.org).

Glossary

Active voice – writing in which the subject of the sentence is carrying out the action. For instance, "Susan wrote the article" versus "The article was written by Susan." The active is almost always preferable

Advertorial – an article that is written on behalf of a company. It looks like an article (though it will be noted as an advertorial) but is paid for as an ad would be

All rights – the publication or client owns all rights including reprints. The author may not sell or reuse the article but does retain the copyright

Assignment – an editor requests a specific article for an agreed-upon fee

Audience – the people reading the article

Bibliography – a list of references used in an article

Bimonthly – every two months

Bio – usually one – three sentences about the person whose name appears in the byline. Often appears at the end of the published article.

Body – the main text of the article

Byline – name of the author appearing with the published work (note: this may be the client's name versus the freelancer)

Caption – a brief description of the content of an image or photo

Circulation – number of subscribers to a publication – may or may not be audited (verified)

Clips – samples of a writer's published work

Consumer publication – magazines in which the content is targeted to consumers versus businesses. Often sold either by subscription or on a newsstand

Contributor's copies – copies supplied by the publisher, usually free, sometimes in lieu of payment

Copy – what you write; content

Copyediting – editing for grammar, punctuation, and accuracy

Copyright – a legal means to protect an author's work

Cover letter – letter (can be hard copy or electronic) that accompanies an article (or other attachment)

Creative brief – usually used by advertising agencies, this is a document that describes the overall project, its goals and components

Deadline – when an assignment is due

Dek – a journalistic term, the second part of a headline; subtitle

Developmental editing - developmental editing refers to editing that aims to improve the content and structure of a manuscript

Draft – a version of an article – usually used when referring to a piece prior to editing

Editorial – an opinion piece; often written by a staff member or editor

Feature – an article, usually with a human-interest twist versus news. It is usually prominently "featured" on the cover and/or the Table of Contents

Editing – to review a piece for grammatical, spelling and other errors in copy and/or content (see copy editing and developmental editing)

Fees – money paid to the writer

Filler – a short item used to "fill" out a page or section in a magazine or newspaper. Many freelancers and reporters start out writing fillers

Flow – used to describe the organization and progression of a piece of writing. A good flow is smooth with logical transitions or worthwhile leaps

Ghostwriter – a person who writes content based on information and content from another person's knowledge or expertise

Guidelines – instructions for writing an article

Hed – journalistic jargon for headline

Hook – a part of a story that engages the readers

Infographic – graphics that tell a story; usually more detailed than most graphics

Kill fee – a fee paid by a publication to an author if their piece is not published. It's usually a fraction of the agreed upon fee and if a kill fee is offered, it should be part of the initial agreement

Lede – journalistic term for opening of the article; a/k/a lead

Manuscript – author's copy

Multiple submissions – when an article (or book manuscript or proposal) is simultaneously submitted to more than one publication/publisher

Nut graf – the paragraph that goes from the lede to the body of the article; a journalistic term

On spec (speculation) – when the author agrees to write and submit an article but the publication reserves the right to accept or reject the piece

One-time rights – rights that allow a publication the right to publish an article one-time and then rights revert back to the writer who can then submit elsewhere

Paraphrasing – to restate a phrase by using other words in order to shorten the passage or make it more comprehensible to the reader. Be careful – it's often a fine line between paraphrasing and quoting. I use "according to" frequently

Payment on acceptance – payment is received when the publication accepts the piece (often after edits)

Payment on publication – payment is received after publication

Peer-reviewed journal – peer-reviewed journals do not have staff writers. Instead, each academic journal has a peer review board - a panel of subject matter experts that decide from a pool of submitted materials which articles are selected and what changes are required

Point of view – the view from which the story is told

Query – also known as a "pitch letter," a query is a letter that sells the idea to an editor

Quotations – a piece of speech or writing from another source. Adequate citation should always be included and quotation marks should be used to separate the quote

Red ink – an editor's changes. The name is taken from when red pens were actually used

Rejection – possible response to a pitch in which the editor declines to use the article

Revision – process of taking a new look at the article (either by the author or the editor) and making appropriate changes based on edits

Run-on sentence – two or more sentences that do not include proper punctuation or connecting words

SASE – self-addressed stamped envelope – use by the editor to return a manuscript – still used in many writer's guidelines but refers to hard copy queries

Sidebar – a short piece (usually around 100 words) that is visually separate from the article and provides supporting information that may not fit easily into the flow of the article

Subhead – ways to separate ideas in an article

Tagline – a byline that appears at the end of the article instead of the beginning and usually includes a sentence or two about the author's qualifications

Tear sheet – page from the actual publication that includes the article

Terms – the agreement details between the author and the publisher

Vertical publications – Usually business-to-business publications targeted towards specific industries or segments within an industry

Unsolicited manuscript – a manuscript that has not been requested

Voice – style, tone and method of writing in a work

Work for hire – most of the work you do will be work for hire – that is, you are being paid to do a specific project but the rights to the piece will remain with your client or the publication

Writer's guidelines – (see Guidelines above)

About the Author:

Ginny Simon, founder of Project Marketing, has been handling public relations and marketing projects for clients for more than 25 years. Ongoing and project assignments include press releases, media contacts, articles, newsletters, and various other writing  assignments. During this period, hundreds of articles have been published on topics ranging from marketing, management, banking, and insurance to legal matters and health care. From features to how-to articles and profiles, these articles have appeared in more than 40 different publications in a variety of industries. They have been written as part of publicity efforts for clients as well as "on-assignment" for regional business publications and national trade magazines. She also helped develop and teach a class on Freelance Writing at a major university.

Ginny has a BA from Boston University and an MBA from Temple University.

She lives in the Philadelphia suburbs with her husband Mike and their very friendly pit bull, Lucy.

Made in the USA
Middletown, DE
21 July 2017